GW01017980

For Blair French, who put me back on the road
and Sally who stayed when the brakes failed.

Contents

Pit

'Geordie' Egleston, 'Cac' Allan,
'Shady' Joe, 'Sloper' Allison.
Once more I squeeze
From the hardening stone of my Grandfather's memory
That sad litany of village epithets.

Jack earned his on the playground gravel,
Tongue too short, called himself Cac,
By fourteen he was caged with the rest of them,
The proud enunciator of John and Joe and Josh
Already sinking into blackness.
Shit sticks in a pit village.

Sixty years back me grandad spoke another language,
The language of onsetters, banksmen and and stonesmen,
The language of Shady, Sloper and Cac,
A language whose core was a rusting nine hundredweight tub,
Their words spinning round it thick as coaldust.

Tommy Heron's father was the pick-sharpener,
And a fine pick-sharpener at that.
They paid for his services themselves,
Paid for pit stockings, pit boots, pit helmets,
Four ounce greaseproof powder packets from the Cabin Man.

Billy Hepple's at his shot-hole, eye out for the firer
Adding extra powder for a bigger fall,
Poor bugger dreamed of dying rich,
At one and six a tub his dream came only halfways true,
The 'place closed', fell in, crushed him.
We all have our euphemisms, our bucket-kicking to console us.

Grandad's the last one left, the final survivor of his District,
'Windy-picks', the new pneumatics
Robbed him of his language.
It was pointless.
Conversation? You couldn't even hear yourself in bye.

Packwalls, quarters, props, girders,
Seams and cages, baulks and canches,
Broken workings.
His cant is failing, words are dying.
I ask him to reclaim them, to dig them from the goaf.

'goaf' : a seam which has been emptied of its coal

Regrouting the Bathroom in the Wrong Century

Somewhere else it's undoubtedly decadent, but not here.
Regrouting the bathroom kind of saps that sensual style,
Robs you of all subcutaneous baroque pretensions.
I'd like to be dissolute, knock back that mythical third bottle
of *Nottage Hill* (on a Tuesday), put on my dandified silk shirt
and paint the town red. But, there's the alarm to set and I don't repair
like I used to.

I'd revalorise my decaying house if the paint brushes
hadn't all contracted alapecia. The TV's on the blink
and my stress-induced pruritus needs creaming. This is the wrong century!
I'm in need of candle-shadows, my body's fat under the strip lighting.
It would seem furtive: bathing with the light off. And besides, the grout's not
    dry.
Give me the telephone number of a reputed firm of interior decorators
and a pocket full of money.

Lucozade Junkie

None of us could spell the rash
of new diseases sweeping through the classes
like a caretaker on Acid.

When I was nine I didn't care,
Knocked about with kids still scabby,
Victims of the 'Chicken Pots'
                    I was a lucozade junkie.

Lacked the cunning of an addict,
Failed in schoolyard jurisprudence,
Children wise to odd behaviour
                    I was a lucozade junkie.

I was nine, I needed fixing,
Hooping cough and Starlit Fever
struck down friends and left me brassed-off
                    I was a lucozade junkie.

Dreamed at night of orange liquid,
Cellophane wrapped around a screw-top bottle
Asked God, by my bed, to bless me with sickness
                    I was a lucozade junkie.

Seeking Puffins

At this bus-stop ledge
Where the treespill cries,
In the pavement race of clutching leaves
I hear again that cliff top scream of gulls.

See the Puffins

and I'm scanning the vertical for banded bills
        sea mouth foaming,
            tongue-tip tasting salt
Father's hands tight around my calves

They nest here

Discounting gulls and guillemots
I am ready to capitulate,
To lose this strange game of hide-and-seek
And then, no more than an arm's length distant
I see it watching,
My eyes meet Puffin eyes - it soars
and I attempt to follow.

Dad flew too...
off the handle; bloody this and that
Saw me spread across the rocks
        smashed
Then, calming, raised his finger to the sky

Do you see it?

he asked me
but the boat was waiting
and we needed to leave.

Evil Writing

and you didn't understand!
excuse my ivel vreitin
for y nevver used it afor * you wrote
The sound of your voice dancing in the phonetics.

Go to the streets outside these walls,
Hold your nosegay tight beneath your chin
Choose at random, ask anyone and they'll tell you
There are things here more *ivel* than sentences,
Daggers under black cark doublets
With points far sharper
Than the corners of your leather-bound octavos.
It's not rhyme that sore-stripes backs,
Not print that puts heads through hempen windows.

The grand hall has a February chill to it,
Someone breathing smoke warms his ass by the fire
You fix his eye, slowly remove the black robe,
dress,
jacket
Then stand still as stone on that scaffold,
Still in your petticoat of crimson velvet,
Still in your bodice red as blood,
Blood from tip to toe,
Still and staring.

And it's not some book they lift then
High above your pale neck as you kneel,
Not shaky spelling that splits bone and severs flesh.

Your whimpering dog scampers back
Confused eyes twitching left and right
Then sits itself down between your bloody pieces
Barking.

* Extract from letter to Sir Frances Knolly written by Mary Queen of Scots, September 1568. Cotton Ms. Caligula C.I., F218 (British Library). Mary was beheaded at Fotheringay Castle on the morning of February 8th 1587.

Other People's Lives

I'm out window shopping for other people's lives
without the necessary time to buy a Bishop
or a fat man cutting meat.
Home rooms are private
nets are up and newly laundered
Sunday's china on the table.

Veiled eyes watch,
I feel them on my skin
Perhaps they have stories I can colonize
perhaps they are merely dusting,
perhaps.

The gift shop window glistens with glazed pigs
and locally carved ornaments
neatly ordered like choirboys on shelves -
off-cuts of the region taken through our doors
to help us hear cathedral bells
in villages deprived of architecture,
houses where we dream of other lives.

Tasteful Neighbourhood

Flats call themselves apartments,
Their ossiferous closets
Well supplied with bone.
Honesty's suspended,
Likewise floors and ceilings.
The pretty people
Are sleeping in tiers
...no springs attached.

Beach

There's a washed-out snap of my brother and I
Playing on the beach you can't play on now,
The sea is blue; the sand, faded yellow.

There are no limp tampons or vicious gulls at the pipe's end
No over-fertilised and foetid seaweed piles
Popping gas that stinks when you inadvertently step on it.

At low tide we'd race down and swim until our feet numbed,
Now you're best advised to wear a wet-suit,
Favour breast-stroke, head well up, lips tight as fists.

Mam wouldn't recognise this place from Adam. *You can smell the sea*
She'd say as we walked down Walker Terrace. And you could,
You'd fill your lungs with it and laugh.

Today the rockpools have a rainbow skin, the scent
Of petrol. And there's no gold you fool, nothing stirring in the stagnant
Stillness. Not even the sidling of a solitary crab.

My brother's children will be banned from here
They won't build castles or throw driftwood for the dog.
The sea is grey, the sand has lost its yellow.

33,000 Feet in 68 Syllables

1

Wild mercury thread
Polygons, right-angled land
Spent curves cutting through.

2

Irregular edge
Creased silk sea, woven waves, boat
V. Cloud-line wake.

3

Water, worn gold-plate
Thin black line, claw, metal crack
Sea-scratch, harbour wall.

4

Limpet ice-spiders
Silver glass urchins. Below,
White elephant skin.

Of Pigeons and People

Before the midday sun
Shaves them off with burnt feet
A grey stubble of pigeons
Huddle on the terracotta rooftop tiles
Preening.

Across the Pont Neuf
An old woman washes
Another week of traffic dirt
From her windows.

Above, the silver foil coating
Of a precisely angled shutter
Trains the early heat inside:
A young couple breakfast
In their redirected rays.

(Toulouse. December 22nd 1993.)

Cheap Hotels

Behind their mendacious entrance halls
          all ticking clocks and polished wood
There are cigarette burns in the bargain-sex bedspreads.

Under ill-fitting polystyrene ceilings
          that grind beneath the beds above
Wardrobes totter on impoverished legs.

Tonight there's only one thing dropping off,
A skew-whiff Latin lady with a low-cut blouse,
She leans a little further on her nail
Exposing mock-canvas in the accelerating sixty watt
                                    shadows.

Signs of madness must be recognised swiftly:
A Sisyphean wish to sleep,
The obsessive reading of encapsulated fire regulations,
An urge to scream just a little louder
          than the couple coming one floor up.

Have no truck with these cheap hotels,
The unnatural desire for malleable wax earplugs
          that they engender.

The Promised View

They promised us the Pyrenees
On a clear day... they whispered
eyes spilling over with memory
in the ensuing reverential silence
                    and, smiling, we imagined mountains.

Today the sky's so blue you could swim in it,
        We've all got twenty twenty vision
                    and we're still imagining mountains.

Tiny skiers smile and wave
Disney snow-crystals softly fall,
To accompany their descent: orchestral glissandos.
The steady swelling harmony of a male-voice choir.
                At their feet
impossible technicolour flowers.

We're all sat contented
Lounging with the lizards on our veranda
Each, their own particular range of peaks

No-one here complains about the view.

Brother

Sunlight filtering through
newly bleached window net,
Cigarette smoke with the tears taken out
My on the threshold of *our*

A father or a doctor,
Something tall and adult speaking
One word, commencing with the cold,
concluding with a snarl:
> *Brother*

About to transcend language,
Just beyond the bedroom door. `

The word is in her arms
They introduce me to it with whispers.
Two abstract syllables assume form
With the slight shift of a towel.

A Nice Man

The fissure widened, stone parted and the sky came in.
Suitably alarmed, we phoned a man who came with glass and glue
Like some harmless double-glazing dealer. *This is nothing
Mate,* he said, sensing my anguish. *Today the sky's a fine shade of blue,
But wait until Winter.* A long silence. We didn't smile.
He left with a renewed appreciation of concrete and shoe leather's
Acoustics. *Just joking,* he muttered as he walked off. For a while
The glass stood up well. We'd almost forgotten it and then the weather
Changed. Wind blew, rain lashed, snow fell: glass cracked.
Alarmed, we phoned the man who brought another man with electrical
    gadgets
He smiled like he'd been too long in front of cameras, said *Sit back,
Relax.* You could see his brow beading with sweat.
Some months later he came back with no jokes, a photograph and plan
Of our cottage. *I'm sorry,* he said to the floor. He really was a nice man.

Two Syllable Debt

We end the meal with spires, rooftops, trees
The sun falls into sharp silhouettes.
I try on his 7$_{3/8ths}$ Panama.
My head's too big, looks funny tilted -
Something to laugh at between rapidly descending
                                        silences.

There are things to go back for,
To sit on planes for,
To travel over the sea and far away for.
He gives me tomatoes in a plastic bag,
If he could grow money
I'd be handed that

...says he'll miss me shouting *Grandad*
from the bedroom window
on a morning after Mass.

I owe him just one word
Two syllables, no more.
To fail when so little is requested
                        and walk away?

There are no clever words left
No metaphors, no quick alliteration,
No 7$_{3/8ths}$ hat to hide under.

Dinosaur Footprints

In the carpet pile, vacuumed indentations
stubborn as dinosaur footprints
reveal the old alignment of his chairs.
They tried to hoover him out then stopped.
Drawers, still full of his elastic band-wrapped habits
Squeal at my intrusion.

Bending to pull a suitcase full of possibilities
from the concealed unpainted skirting board
my empty hands momentarily touch the weight of his distance.
The ephemera of such absence bursts from cupboards,
This is still his house, there is much to be undone.

At the Study window - a neglected garden looking up,
The lawn already buckled with the pressure of his hidden bulbs
Pale green fingers scratch through cold earth
Clutch, once more, at the light he left behind.

Fields for Sea

In Melbourne
the weather is hot.
It sits you down in the shade like a baby,
it liquifies the horizon of roads and pavements
And gran,
gran on an outing under her hat
is mistaking fields of grass
for sea.
They correct her error jovially,
put her failing sights to rights.
I hear her staccato laugh,
she shakes her head
as if she knew the answer all along,
could not for a moment understand how
she'd been so silly as to…
fields for sea indeed!
And inside she is shaking.

Dear God
in Melbourne
let grass be water one time for her
let rolling green break on her shore
let it gently lap the living flesh of her feet.

A Drink Without Bubbles

I remember when it was different
When we tore at our words
like close-to-Christmas unexpected parcels.

A light scattering of grey coats the table,
Fall-out from the ashtray epicentre
Of our conversation-of-sorts.

The browning edge of a shark's fin lemon-slice surfaces
Above your abandoned Cola
Now totally devoid of fizz.

I watched its ice cube melting
As we talked and drank
Inadequately.

It is the end now
They are wiping our reflections into the glass;
New silences have been conquered.

We talked,
Tested new sentences,
With words as hollow as mailshot promises.

The Small Hours

It's during them that you begin to recognise it for a misnomer,
There's nothing petite, paltry, undersized
In their volatile seconds, ticking away the unfamiliar absence
                                                    of traffic.

They're *when-the-ache-comes-back*, the between-analgesic hours
Viewless windows metamorphose, their constant repeating floral monotony
Closes in on the sick with their alien words, their sutures and their
                                                    haematomas.

They're the slow-motion kill in a Peckinpah movie
Played over and over; the time when the maximum dose
Gives minimal relief and the pain is shot in
                                        technicolour.

It's an Andy Warhol movie, a single housefly on the wall of time
Static, silent above the unhealed entry wound where a nail's been pliered
    out
of the wall. My room is a box. The minutes in my box are
                                                    protracted.

Room

I imagined us on an aerial photograph,
A strange druidic marking in the field,
Puzzled archaeologists pondering the significance
Of six beds circled round a rough patch
                              of scorched earth.

That night the walls were constantly shifting,
Sometimes it seemed like you could
Press your nose against them,
But the faint glow of headlights
Lit further distances, new boundaries
                              to my room.

And the ceiling was flickering,
Light-dots pulsing in black.

I slept well.

Rain woke me,
At first a fine mist, then heavy drops.
There was no need to struggle with cracked tiles,
Or labour with filler and tubes of sealant,
So I lay still, damp and contented
As my friends ran for cover.

DB 16

Fifteen others first,
as used as the bobbing prophylactics
- you followed -
It's not a clean death in this water
Filthy keen to enter every orifice as
it sucks you
            under.

We hook you, photograph you,
tag you, freeze you
efficient as your
final act.

No personality rises
like a sodden Phoenix
from the Thames this time,
           just flesh and hair and
                   silence.

No clues,
No answers,
No final solution.
We bury our questions,
Return to our duties,
It's time to name another number.

Beware of the Language

We are early,
The road has not been watered.
Through dust, the fretted stone of temples,
An incunabular desire to stay hatching.
The exhaust is shot,
We rumble like a Harley.
Bewildered monkeys scream from waste bins
Their upper lips just rolled white slivers.

A dog,
A big dog,
All lolling tongue and spittle
Chases furiously into our maelstrom.

She has seen the fear in my eyes
            There are no bad dogs here
An unequivocal response, a smile,
My sybaritic fortnight is undamaged.

We're in the jeep again
Slowing for cattle.
Her fruit scatters as teeth sink into thigh,
With a simple shake of its head
A pigeon-piece of flesh tears free
            You lied
I scream with the monkeys
As dust laps blood.
            You lied
            There are no bad dogs
            Remember?
            Do you remember?
She thinks,
Explains that *that* is not a good dog,
Shrugs.

            The jeep is heading for the harbour.
            If you come here please watch out for the dogs,
            Beware of the language.

Closure

Let not the pit shut her mouth upon me *[1]
Four words too long for the Durham miners.
Walking down the road to foreshift
Tom and Billy Fleetham and the road still wet,
Sizzled like bacon when lightning struck tarmac:
A half century; nothing but a bait stand *[2] when he told it,
But the stories have all closed down,
And it's me left salvaging at Bank.

Driving full tubs to the flat and empty ones back,
A stable-lad with chalk in his pockets
Drawing ponies on his shovel back
Then digging them off again. Lives measured in laid-outs *[3]
It didn't make a ha'puth if the blue cap leapt, *[4]
If you crawled through water or your lamp smoked up
If you couldn't see a hand before your face with dust,
As long as you were winning out in the Third West Flatt
And the fire in the Undermanager's office was roaring.

The coffin's on the trestles and the men have their caps off,
Coxhoe band's in Main Street playing hymns.
A tune for a life and crepe around the Gala banner,
A write-up in the Minutes Book, a single district closed.
They said they wished the shaft was filled in
And the farmer had his fields back,
Stood silent in the riding shaft, worked wet down the Hutton.
A shilling less a shift, *[5] picked their way through hitches, *[6]
Shovelled stone in the kibble, *[7] dug a deeper hole.

When fires and inundations were forgotten by the children,
Grandad handed me a hundred years contained in eighty pages.
Witton Lodge, Sherburn Hill, Harraton, New Shildon,
Waterhouses, Deaf Hill, Middridge, Thrislington.
Closure. Closure. Closure. Closure.
A table of events and a longer list of lives lost,
Pain reduced to numbers, totalled in the sump. *[8]
He's on the cover with his head behind a banner, *[9]
And under his suit there's pit dust in his lungs.

Ten years later I followed him down the hill past Elvet Bridge,
Squeezing *Gresford* through brass tubes as the rain came down.
Between marches we kept step to the Big Drum, blew spit from our
   instruments.
All those resolutions, amendments, pamphlets, pledges,
Delegates, chairmen, overmen, workers - and to what end?
The Pit Head baths are dry. Sacriston banner's of historical interest.
No doubt they'll devote a slim volume to it.

*1   Psalm 69:15
*2   *bait stand* - short period of time allocated during a shift for the miners to eat their *bait*
        (lunch)
*3   *laid-outs* - when the contents of a tub were emptied the coal was separated from the
        stones   which were then placed in boxes of fixed sizes (threepenny, sixpenny, a
        shilling) called *laid-outs*. Once filled, the value of the *laid-outs* was deducted from your
        'note' (paynote)
*4   *blue cap* - it often made no difference if the 'blue cap' on the pit lamp's flame 'peaked'
        i.e. taken as an indication that there was gas in the vicinity - this warning sign was often I
        ignored
*5   *a shilling less a shift* - at the conclusion of the 1926 General Strike and lock-out the
        miners lost to the coal-owners' demands and were forced to work an extra hour per
        shift for a shilling less pay
*6   *hitches* - sections of stone in the coal seams
*7   *kibble* - a *kibble* is a three-sided tub designed to be easily filled with stones
*8   *sump* - the *sump* is a large hole (below the boards where the cage which lowered the
        miners stopped) at the bottom of the shaft
*9   *behind a banner* - when Durham had a coalfield, once a year on 'Big Meeting Day',
        bands marched through the city behind their colliery banners